Costume Reference 3

Jacobean, Stuart and Restoration

Costume Reference 3

Jacobean, Stuart and Restoration

MARION SICHEL

Publishers   PLAYS, INC.   Boston

First published 1977
© text and illustrations 1977, Marion Sichel

First American edition published by Plays, Inc. 1977

Library of Congress Cataloging in Publication Data

Sichel, Marion.
    Costume Reference.
        Includes bibliographies and indexes.
CONTENTS: v. 1 Roman Britain and the Middle Ages –
v. 2. Tudors and Elizabethans – v. 3. Jacobean, Stuart and
Restoration
    1. Costume – Great Britain – History.
    I. Title
GT 730.S48   1977   391'.00941
76-54466   0-8238-0214-0 (vol. 3)

Printed in Great Britain

Contents

Introduction   7

Before the Fall: 9

James I (1603–25) and Charles I (1625–49)

Roundheads and Restoration: 35

Commonwealth (1649–60)

Charles II (1660–85)

James II (1685–89)

William and Mary (1689–1702)

Glossary   62

Bibliography   68

Index   69

Introduction

In England the seventeenth century was a period of profound conflict between the aristocratic order and the now powerful middle classes. In Europe too we can see a similar conflict between the more severe burghers of the Netherlands and the increasingly aggressive activities of France on the one hand and the declining power of Spain on the other. Needless to say these tensions were reflected in the styles of clothing adopted.

James I's reign (1603–25) represented the last expression of the old stable Elizabethan order. Costume tended to reflect this continuation of tradition in the stiffer, highly adorned fashions of Elizabeth's reign. Here the Spanish sense of formality still lingers in the slim corseted waistlines, rich materials and jewelled decoration.

Clothes are an expression of the age, and this was the age of a fast rising and influential France, ably and ambitiously guided by those two formidable statesmen, cardinals Richelieu and Mazarin. With Charles I's accession in 1625 and his marriage to the French Henrietta Maria French taste began to dominate. Gone was the bombast and stiffness of the old Spanish style; cast aside was the farthingale and stomacher; in came softer folds and materials, looser-fitting clothes, higher waists and more pronounced décolletage; lace and ribbons were the preferred decoration rather than precious stones and rich embroidery.

This style, commonly known as 'Cavalier', has come to be a by-word for self-assured elegance and is particularly well known through the portraits of Sir Anthony van Dyck (who, of course, is remembered in fashion by 'Vandyck' collars, beards or edging).

Men particularly dressed with a wonderful sense of grace, favouring softer materials such as velvet, silk and pliable leathers with looser-fitting jackets, sleeves and breeches.

Feminine dress also changed under the influence of the new mode from France, but the degree of change was less radical when compared with their menfolk. Décolletage was more daring, sometimes completely exposing the breasts. Softer curls and tresses were favoured rather than the hats and more formal hairstyles of their Elizabethan forebears. Skirts hung full and loose and often open in front to show the multiple folds of the petticoat.

The Commonwealth (1649–60), although of a revolutionary nature politically, was not as innovatory in dress. The mistake is often made in assuming that suddenly everyone dressed in the severe style of the Puritans. The leaders of the Protectorate (and Cromwell is a very good example) came from the same social background as their Royalist opposition and tended to dress in a modified Cavalier style.

The restoration of the Stuarts, with the return of Charles II from exile at the Court of Louis XIV in 1660, inevitably brought with it an even stronger French influence which expressed itself in an extravagant gaiety and flamboyance of dress which stood in marked contrast to the true elegance of Charles I's reign. Now there was a fascination with frippery – ribbons, bows, ruffles and tassels bedecked the fashionable and the French rage for wigs on men established itself in England.

As the century wore on into the reigns of James II (1685–89) and William and Mary (1689–1702) fashions become more sedate and, interestingly, one sees the start of the 'suit' which, with modifications, has survived to our own times.

Female fashion changed less throughout the whole century than did men's and this later period saw only relatively minor adaptations of earlier Stuart styles. The small-waisted look which had begun to establish itself during the Commonwealth made a reappearance, whilst, generally, French influence still held sway. In fact in Paris at this time one can see evidence of a highly organized fashion industry which looks forward to the modern *couturier*. Indeed two full-sized dolls, dressed in the latest modes *(Les Poupées Fameuses)*, were sent to London each month.

Before the Fall:
James I (1603–25) and Charles I (1625–49)

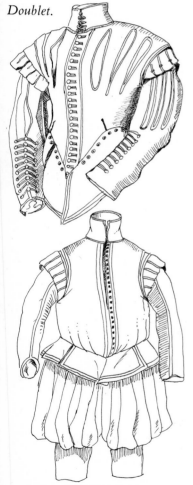

Doublet.

Earlier style doublet with trunks and canions.

Men

DOUBLET

The term 'doublet' for the principal body garment was used until the third decade of the century (c.1670), when it was replaced and thereafter called the 'coat'.

The earlier style from the late 1590s to about 1630 was the long waisted, close-fitting style, stiffened with whale bone, the front part being lined with stiffening such as canvas and buckram. The overhanging pointed padding in the centre front of the doublet (the *peascod*) was now becoming un-fashionable, although it persisted in varying degrees of 'overhanging', sometimes round with a slight dip in the front or drooping to a sharp point in the front.

Coming into fashion also was the *belly-piece* (from about c.1620 and continued in fashion until c.1665). The belly-piece was formed by two triangular sections of thick stiff material, which were sewn on either side at waist level, making a centre front fitting into the pointed *girdlestead* (waistline) and coming half-way up the centre front.

The skirt of the doublet from the 1590s to c.1610 flared out from the round waist, the *basque* being formed from the separate short square tabs, about eight in number, with a slight overlap. From 1610 until 1630 the tabs were cut deeper and the two central tabs came to a long sharp point in front, and either slightly overlapped or came edge-to-edge. After 1620 a further lengthening of the tabs was brought about because the waist of the doublet became higher and, in consequence, the tabs were reduced in number, to about six. After the 1630s the waist became even higher and the tabs were further reduced in number to four, two at the back and two in the front.

The *collar* was high and deep and, sometimes, although rarely, cut with a V-shape vent at the throat. The fastening was usually with button and loops, unlike the doublet which was closed with hooks and eyes or 'points' (lace or ribbon), or with buttons and button-holes down the centre front.

Sleeves were usually plain, straight and close fitting, although on occasions the puffed-out style around the shoulders and elbows could be seen, but this was not in common use. Projecting welts which encompassed the sleeve at the shoulder, called 'wings' were worn, narrow at first, becoming broader from *c*.1610 and remaining in fashion until the late 1620s although completely outmoded by *c*.1640. Sleeves were often open from the wrist to the elbow and were closed with buttons and button-holes similar to the doublet's. A short buttoned slit in the sleeve was sometimes used as a pocket. During the period 1620–35, sleeves were usually paned from the shoulder to the elbow, which revealed the full sleeve of the shirt or a coloured lining, the sleeve often being fastened up the back seam by buttons.

The doublet from *c*.1600–20 had short symmetrical designs with slashings and pinking. Later, from *c*.1620 to *c*.1630 the slashings and panes became longer and were worn by the fashionable on the chest and the back, usually in vertical slits. Through these slits either the full shirt was pulled, or coloured lining was seen. This, however, fell from favour in the 1640s.

Following the shape of the waistline was the fashionable narrow *sword belt*, with highly decorated hangers supporting the sword. In *c*.1625 the fashion altered and the waistbelt was superseded by the *baldrick*, an elaborately ornamental shoulder belt.

In the early 1640s the doublet began to show very positive structural changes and the corset shape was replaced. The whole appearance was now one of a relaxed, easy-fitting style. Gone was the heavy padding and stiffening was confined to the belly-piece which was still retained in fashion. Eyelets, used for securing the hose to the doublet ('trussing the points'), although still present, served purely as decorative ornamentation without any further functional usage.

The skirt of the doublet became very high waisted and the tabs became deep and square but usually pointed in the front. This soon lost favour, however, and by *c*.1635 the front tabs were squared off level with the others, now being six in

Doublet open at centre chest with shirt showing through.

number.

The *collar* remained stiff and high-standing, keeping the haughty appearance so often seen in the contemporary portraits of the fashionable figures of the period.

The doublet still retained the centre-fastening down the front from the neck to the waistline with buttons and button holes but the fashionable trend was to allow the doublet to be left open from about the centre of the chest level to show the full, embroidered silk shirt beneath.

Sleeves followed the newer style and were loose; no longer close fitting as in the previous fashion. They were closed at the wrist by buttons which were placed down the seam at the back, or they finished just below the elbow with a deep turned-back cuff; the full shirt sleeve came down to the wrist. Another style of sleeve was full from the shoulder to the elbow and was paned, then closed to the wrist.

The *shoulder wings* were now very small, sometimes merely a welt, and by the early 1640s had finally disappeared.

The *belt,* which had become broader, was often discarded in favour of the baldrick.

From the late 1640s to the 1670s the doublet became very short, unpadded and unlined, with only a slight stiffening in the front.

The *doublet skirt* was, by now, a mere tabbed border, the doublet being so short that there was a gap between the doublet and the breeches, which was filled in by a volume of protruding shirt. The *breeches* either hung from the hips or were secured via eyelet rings under the shirt. The high standing collar remained, often stiffened with buckram, which supported the standing or falling collar.

Waistcoats became fashionable and were worn as an under-doublet garment.

JACKET AND JERKIN

The *jerkin* which had been so popular began to lose its popularity and finally became unfashionable by the early 1630s. It had followed the change of fashion of the doublet, following the same changes of pattern, but with, more often than not, a longer skirt. Sleeves were invariably absent, with edging of the armhole covered by the wings; the hanging sleeves were false and were for decoration only.

The military style *buff coat,* which was of leather hide treated with oil, became very popular for civilian wear. It was close-fitting, with a high waistline, the deep skirt reaching down to just below hip length, and overlapped in the front with slits to the waist at the back, and sometimes also at the sides. The rounded neckline was collarless, this being hidden by the large falling-band collar which covered the shoulders.

Buttons, or lacing fastened the coat down the centre front to the waistline and sometimes closely arranged points were used. Although usually sleeveless, tubular appendages were occasionally attached and worn as hanging sleeves. A sleeve of a soft material could be attached or even sewn on under the narrow welt wing (giving the impression of an under-garment doublet) and these were often slit down on the upper seam to show the full shirt sleeve beneath; the cuff of the coat sleeve usually ended with matching lace similar to the falling collar. Up to the early 1620s a loose thigh-length overcoat was worn known as the *mandilion*. This was placed on over the head and buttoned down the chest, with sleeves of the sham hanging variety.

OVERCOAT

A more popular overcoat was the *cassock,* a loose garment, which was tent-like widening gradually to the hem with a vent up the back. It was a hip length garment up to the early 1620s, after which skirts became longer to thigh length. The fastening was down the centre front, either by lace or buttons. The narrow standing collar, which was popular until the 1620s finally disappeared and either no collar was present, or a flat, turned-down collar was worn, this re-maining in fashion until the 1660s. The sleeves were fairly loose to the wrist and had a turned-back cuff.

The *gaberdine*, worn as an overcoat, was a large long loose garment, with extra-wide sleeves used by all sections of the people in various guises and by both sexes in inclement weather.

CLOAKS

Up to the late 1660s the cloak was an essential part of the fashionable man's attire. They came in various styles and for a variety of uses, such as riding, travelling and for inclement weather. The most popular were circular, usually matching the underlying garments of the doublet and breeches. The length also varied from very long to the ankles, to very short thigh length. Surviving from the late 1570s to the late 1670s was the *manteau à la reitre,* a popular form of French cloak long to the knees and worn with or without a collar. If a collar was present it was usually a flat-to-the-

Peasant style, c.1620. The
man is wearing a thigh-length
jerkin made of coarse material.
The knee-breeches, Venetian-
type, were worn with rolled-up
stockings. The hat is a 'sugar
loaf' style. The girl wears a
white linen chemise with a
square neck and a laced bodice
worn over. The overskirt is
gathered up around the waist.
A white coif or cap is covered by
a straw hat.

shoulder type, forming a square at the back, or the earlier style was the deep shoulder cape which fell to elbow length.

The cloak fastening varied with the taste of the wearer. Sometimes it was left unfastened and slung over the body and allowed to fall in loose folds or fastened at the neck only and worn over both shoulders, or worn over one shoulder and gathered up and carried over the arm. The neck was usually hidden under the lace or linen collar, which was worn over the outside.

The earlier *Spanish cloak* fell from favour in the early 1620s. This was the short cape type with the fitted pointed hood. The *Dutch cloak*, although not so fashionably popular, remained in vogue until the 1640s. This was similar to the Spanish cloak, differing only in the attached sleeves and being slightly looser fitting.

Mandilion (in fashion 1570–1620s).

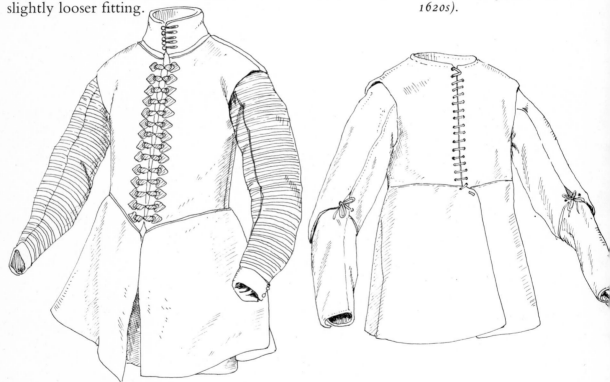

Leather buff coat, c.1625. The high stand up collar was fastened with buttons and loops. From the neckline to the waist fastening was by metal clasps. The leather coat was sleeveless, but had soft material sleeves attached. The sides and back were open from the waistline.

Leather buff coat, c.1635. Fastening was from the high collarless neckline to the waist with lacing. The sleeves were short to the elbow, with a softer leather sleeve emerging, reaching wrist level. The buff coat also had openings at the sides and back from the waist.

14

Cassock or Gabardine

NECK AND WRISTWEAR

The *ruff,* which had been so popular in the previous century, remained until the late 1640s being worn alongside the more fashionable standing- and falling-band types. Larger ruffs completely disappeared after about 1620. The 'falling ruff', which was formed by several layers sewn onto a neckband, was closed all round and fastened by band strings, remained in fashion until the early 1640s.

The *standing band,* fashionable for a quarter of a century, of Spanish origin and called a *golilla,* was cut in a semi-circular shape and stood up round the back of the head; the straight edge in the front was fastened at the throat with band strings, this being supported with a wire frame known as an *under-propper.* The band was made from linen or lawn, stiffened with starch and dyed in a colour to suit the wearer. This same type of band could also be worn without the wire support and turned down over the shoulders, with a V-shape at the throat.

The *falling band* was similar to the modification of the standing band but was purpose-made to lay flat, previously it was a small turned down collar, but on its fashionable revival, it was increased in size and became very popular.

The wrists were also decorated with either the hand ruff or ruffle and was made like a miniature ruff, or handfall, which was a turned-back starched cuff, often doubled to add thickness and matched the neck band.

HOSE AND BREECHES

The evolution of men's leg wear in the seventeenth century was from various types of trunk hose to breeches. The term 'hose' (more like a modern pair of women's tights) gradually came to mean 'stockings', instead of the complete nether garment.

The standing band (gollila) style made of a transparent material and edged with lace, c.1612.

Broad lace falling-band collar.

Long cloak to the knees, both Spanish and Dutch type with falling collar.

Compound ruff with flattened figure-of-eight set.

Trunk hose with canions remained the most popular fashion and stayed in vogue from the late 1570s to the early 1620s. These were in various styles, stiff, long and short, and all rather cumbersome. The stiff type were tight at the waist, falling stiffly downwards and outwards, being stuffed and padded into a hard shape, finishing about mid-thigh, and fitted with short canions (see Glossary).

The short version was gathered at the waist and similar in shape to the stiff type but with longer canions. The longer style was gathered at the waist and fell in folds, giving it the appearance of very large full breeches. Fitted just above the knee to canions, they finished below the knee. The padded protrusion, which was previously a part of the trunk hose, and called a cod-piece, had now disappeared, and was replaced with the front vent which was covered by a loose flap, or closed with buttons.

Eyelet holes on the skirt at the waist of the doublet had tags of ribbon which were passed through holes on the waistband of the trunk hose, thus serving as decoration on the outside of the doublet.

Breeches came in various forms, *Venetian, slops, cloak bag, Spanish hose* and *open breeches* for example. *Venetians* stayed in fashion from the last century to *c,*1620 and were a form of knee breeches gathered at the waist, padded round the hips, narrowing down to just below the knee where they were closed with buttons or ribbon ties.

Galligaskins and *slops* were of the same period being very similar in shape, wide and loose fitting. The *cloak bag* breeches (*c*.1620 to 1630) were again similar, being gathered at the waist not quite as full as previous styles and shaped in, and highly decorated with points and braided embroidery.

Spanish hose or *long-legged* breeches were, as their name implies, long to just below the knee from a high waistline. They were full in the seat and were shaped to the figure, close fitting to the hips and falling to just below the knees, where they were either closed with garters and ends tied into large bows, or they were left like modern shorts to overhang the stockings. The centre vent was again like the more modern trouser flies but with exposed buttons. At about hip level were vertical slits or 'placket holes', which were the forerunner of modern pockets. *Open* breeches were again similar to Spanish hose, but these became wider and were the forerunner of the most extreme fashion of the petticoat breeches.

LEG WEAR

Stockings, lavishly embroidered, were an important feature in leg wear and indeed the fashionable man was concerned about the shape of the leg, often padding the calf to give a better line.

Although they were still tailored, the fashion for knitted stockings in either wool, thread or silk became general, although poor people wore stockings which were partly knitted and partly tailored. Embroidered clocks were designed to reach to calf height.

Garters were often worn to keep stockings in place. They were worn just below the knees and consisted of ribbons tied in bows. *Boot hose,* made of a thicker material such as linen, popular until the 1680s, were a kind of overstocking worn to protect the thinner stockings. The tops had decorative borders, often brightly coloured or laced and could be turned over the boot tops.

Stirrup hose worn throughout the century, were used as protection when horse riding and were similar to long overstockings without soles, but with a strap beneath to hold them down.

SHOES AND BOOTS

Until about 1630 all shoes and boots were fairly rounded in the toe later becoming more squared. Heels, made of either wood or leather, began to become popular in the 1600s, but before then, cork wedge heels were worn, from *c*.1595–1620. Cork was also used to make soles thicker. The early heels were not high but soon became more shapely and elegant the higher they rose.

Shoes were mainly made of leather and Spanish leather, known as 'cordovan', gave its name to shoemakers who were known as 'cordwainers'. These shoes were invariably open-sided, the uppers ending in a tongue with ankle straps secured by ribbons. Until *c.*1615 the tops of the shoes were slashed to allow stockings or coloured shoe linings to be seen.

Low-topped shoes became more fashionable with heels of varying heights, from very flat to about 5cm and placed in various different positions, as the modern standard position had not yet been determined.

Shoe roses, very commonly worn on most shoes, varied greatly. They were in various colours and although they started unpretentiously, became very elaborate and large. Made of ribbon loops, lace or leather they were either in sharp contrast or matched the shoe colour. Rosettes, often pre-manufactured, large and decorative, could also be made of silk and were often jewelled.

Slashings gradually went out of favour and shoe vamps became plainer and higher, with high tabs to accommodate the elaborate roses.

Pumps, with thin soles, were often in velvet and were worn by footmen as part of their attire.

Startups, worn mainly by country people, were of a tougher leather and were laced or fastened with buckles reaching above the ankles.

Well-cut *boots* were mainly worn for riding until about 1610, when they became popular wear for gentlemen until the 1660s.

Boots, made of soft leather, were close fitting, lacing up on the outside. They could be thigh length and fastened to the breeches by points. The tops could be folded down when the *buskins* (see Glossary) had cup-shaped tops. These tops became more pronounced after *c.*1648, the boots becoming shorter with tops known as *bucket tops.*

The *Bucket boot* (destined to be popular well into the next century) was of a funnel shape, the tops being ornamented with ribbon knots. The deep tops, as well as the boots themselves, were made of a firm leather and lined in beige or white linen. They were stiffened inside for rigidity but were allowed to form folds around the ankles, as this was considered stylish. White was a very popular colour for a while, including the lace inside the boot tops, which sometimes held secret pockets concealing perfume pads, gloves, letters and even a pistol.

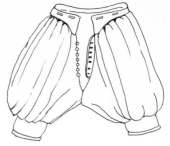

Hose with front vent.

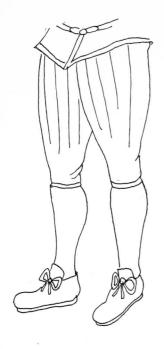

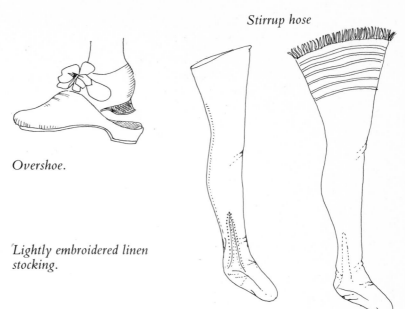

Stirrup hose

Overshoe.

Lightly embroidered linen stocking.

A large piece of leather fastened the stirrup leathers over the front of the instep. The toes were deep and square with a thick welted sole and the heels were also broad and thick.

Spur leathers were broad straps which became so large that they eventually spread over the foot. Spurs were worn by the fashionable, for walking as well as riding, from *c.*1610–1660. *Pantoffles*, were a type of overshoe or mule worn in good road conditions, and were similar in design to their bad-weather relations, galoshes and clogs.

Gamashes were leggings made of a material and fastened by buttoning, whilst *cockers* (leggings), worn mainly in the country, were made of leather.

HEADWEAR

A popular style was the *copotain*, with its high conical crown and flat or slightly turned-up brim. It was invariably worn at a backward angle.

Another style that was worn until the 1640s was a large fairly high-crowned hat, either flat or rounded on top, with the brim usually cocked. After *c.*1620 this brim became very wide.

Hatbands were made of silk cord or ribbon and could be twisted with buttons or feathers, mainly ostrich, also worn as adornment.

Caps ceased to be popular attire, although one type, with a soft crown and small brim was worn by older men, whilst a flat beret type cap, with a narrow brim, was worn mainly by

Copotain hat.

shopkeepers. After about 1640, they were only worn for livery.

The *Monmouth cap,* worn mainly by soldiers and sailors, as well as the Welsh, as its name implies, was a tall, round crowned, brimless cap worn until the mid-century.

Nightcaps, often made of brocade and fine materials, were deep crowned with turned-up brims. The upper part was made in four pieces and, when joined, formed a dome shape.

Monmouth cap.

HAIRSTYLES AND BEARDS

At the beginning of the century, hair was relatively short, but by 1620 longer hair had become more popular with ringlets falling on to the collar. When the hair became really long it was parted at the back and allowed to fall over the shoulders. By the 1630s a fringe had become popular and was often brushed to one side.

Beards and *moustaches* were still popular in the first half of the century. Moustaches were waxed and pointed upwards, whilst beards were mainly short and curly, or in the pointed style seen so often in Vandyke's paintings and in fact bearing his name. Inevitably, it was a style bound to go out of fashion after the fall of Charles I, its most well-known wearer.

Men's and women's hair followed the same trends; when women's hair became longer, the men also grew theirs. As hair became longer, beards became less popular except with the older professional men.

High-crowned hat with cocked brim.

Puritans were clean shaven and had short hair; some of the extremists even had their hair cropped close to the head, and hence their nickname – Roundheads.

Hair at the start of the century was generally short, worn to the tops of the ears and later longer and straight, with the ends slightly curled.

Royalists, by comparison, wore their hair extremely long, full and curly, with ringlets falling to the shoulders and sometimes tied with ribbons and bows at the ends.

A *lovelock,* which was a lock of hair tied with a ribbon and brought to the front, became fashionable and lasted until *c.*1680. A bow or rosette could be worn with this style for decoration.

ACCESSORIES

Gloves with gauntlets were worn mainly up to the 1620s and 1630s. The gauntlet part was made of six to eight parts and ended in a fringe or scalloped edge above the wrists.

Plain gloves without decoration were often made in soft

Long shoulder length hair worn with the vandyke moustache and T beard, after Charles I, c.1635.

Typical helmet worn by the troops during the Civil War, 1642–51.

Glove, c.1620. The gauntlet and around the thumbs was heavily embroidered, the gauntlet being edged with a gold fringe.

leathers, with a small turned-down cuff revealing the coloured lining.

Perfumed gloves were very fashionable and could be worn or just carried.

Mittens, with just a finger and thumb compartment, were made with gauntlets.

Purses were made in a variety of shapes, often heavily embroidered and tasselled at the ends. Purses were closed either by drawstrings or metal snap fastenings.

Fine, large lace-edged *handkerchiefs* were carried; some had buttons or tassels at the corners for ornamentation.

Muckinders were more practical, being made of linen. They were used as handkerchiefs mainly by the working classes, or as table napkins.

Scarves made their appearance in about 1580 and were worn for practicability as well as ornamentation. *Muffs,* made of satin or silk and later of fur, were quite small until the 1630s when they became larger and were either hung from a ribbon around the neck or carried in the hand.

Fashionable upper-class men used perfume, make-up and face patches. They frequently dyed their hair, added false pieces, or wore wigs, curling irons to wave the hair were also used.

Rings were popular, as were chains on which could be worn pendants or lockets worn around the neck.

Earrings on either both or one ear became fashionable and continued to be so until the mid century.

The first quarter of the century saw little or no change in women's dress; there were slight modifications, but little else and to a large extent Elizabethan styles prevailed.

Within the first half of the century changes began to take place and there were two main fashions, 'old' Spanish and 'new' French worn. Although basically the same, the dress consisted of a bodice, a petticoat (previously called a kirtle) and the gown. From *c*.1625 the changes in fashion began to develop and the gown, which had previously been used as an overgarment, now became an integral part of the costume.

BODICE

The bodice or 'body' was worn with a farthingale in the first decade of the century by all fashonable people, but thereafter was, on occasions, worn without until, by about 1625 it was finally discarded. During this early period the waistline was high with a slight point in the front, the low-necked bodice was close fitting and stiffened or 'busked'. The waistline was basqued with a double layer of tabs which could be squared or scalloped. The bodice was fastened down the centre front by lacing, buttoning or ties of ribbon bows. Worn over the bodice was the 'fill-in' or *stomacher*, a triangular-shaped piece of canvas or pasteboard, the apex pointing downwards and the straight edge sometimes being slightly curved, giving a low décolletage effect. This stomacher was usually covered with the matching material of the sleeves and in contrast with the bodice. The very low décolletage remained in fashion for some 50 years, being especially popular among unmarried women which lead the author of *The English Gentleman and English Gentlewoman* (1641) to exclaim: 'Eye those rising mounts, your displayed breasts, with what shameless art they wooe the shamefast passenger.' For others the décolletage was filled in or covered by a fully gathered shirt or chemise which had a standing collar, edged with lace; drapings of lace in a type of shawl across the shoulders fastened in front forming a V-shape or with a transparent material wrapped round the neck.

Bodice sleeves followed very much the earlier styles, the *cannon sleeves* from the late 1550s continued in vogue until the 1620s; these were large at the shoulders with a 'kick up' effect, then tapered down to fit closely at the wrist where they ended with a small hand ruff or a laced turn-back and, where

Farthingale.

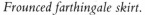
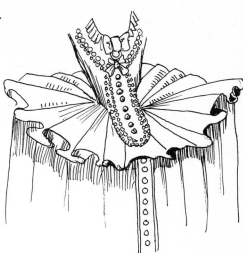

The gown costume.

fashion demanded, both would be worn together. These sleeves were padded and stiffened with wire or whalebone. Shoulder wings were often to be seen in the form of rolls which supported the large sham hanging sleeves. The *leg-of-mutton* type sleeve had a very brief period of popularity, being both cumbersome and heavy with a series of padded, slashed and puffed-out sections running the length of the arm.

Ribbon *girdle belts* were still in fashion to support the pomander, fan or mirror.

JACKET

The jacket was a copy of the male doublet and remained popular throughout the first quarter of the century sometimes being worn in place of the bodice. It was close fitting and only lightly stiffened and flared from the waist in a short skirt which finished round the hips in a straight line. Worn without a collar, the neckline sloped to a plunging V-shape in the front, revealing the breasts (especially for the unmarried). Normal closure was by buttons, hooks and eyes or ribbon ties down the centre front. The sleeves were straight and close fitting to the arm, ending with a small turn-back cuff, slit at the back and buttoned. A hand ruff was always present at the wrist.

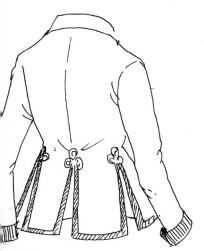

Female jacket similar to male.

SKIRT

The appearance of the skirt was governed by the underlying structure of the petticoat or farthingale. The large structures of the previous century were becoming very unfashionable and early on in the new century they became much smaller.

23

The *wheel-type farthingale* which became unfashionable in the first decade was, as its name suggests, a wired wheel-shape which was placed around the waist, spreading out over the hips, the front and the back, with the front tilted downwards and the back tilted upwards, the main characteristic of this type of farthingale. To fit this contraption the skirt was made tub-shaped being gathered at the waist, laid over the 'wheel' and then allowed to fall down to ankle length. To conceal the join of skirt and bodice and outer-wheel shape, a frounced (stiffened) basque or short skirt, not unlike an enlarged ruff, was secured at the waist. To accentuate the tilt of the farthingale a padded roll, the *bum roll*, not unlike a modern life-belt, with a gap in front fastened with ties, was worn. This was large at first but gradually became smaller after 1615 and later was often worn without the farthingale, giving a tub-shaped skirt effect. Most skirts had the inverted V-shape opening in the front, these on the farthingale skirts were filled in with a forepart, which was secured to the underskirt. Later it became popular to follow the earlier fashion of the 1590s bunching up the sides to reveal an embroidered under-petticoat.

GOWN

The gown as an overgarment remained in popular use until the 1620s becoming old fashioned and rarely worn after this date, but occasionally worn by the elderly up to the 1640s. The neck line had either a small standing collar, the revers or lapel forming a wide V-shape in the front or at the back. The type of fastening was left very much to individual taste; it could be completely open without any form of fastening, secured at the neck only and allowed to remain open all the way down, or closed with an arrangement of buttons and loops from the neckline to the hem. Occasionally, it was secured simply with a sash which encircled the waist.

Sleeves were optional and when present were either straight and short, open in the front seam, often used as hanging sleeves, or were open from the top of the shoulder and used only as hanging sleeves. Wings of various types were always present with or without sleeves. When worn in the home as a négligée the gown developed coat sleeves about 1640.

From 1625 to the 1650s the whole costume was referred to as the gown. The bodice was short-waisted and, more popularly, with a basque which tended to follow the style of the male doublet, the tabs or skirt being deep, often joined together. The newer styles could be closed either at the back

24

LEFT: *c.*1693. Close fitting bodice with stomacher front. The underskirt was with a reversed flounce. Short sleeves and buttoned up cuffs. Neckwear was a steinkirk, and the headdress a fontange. The lady on the horse is wearing the fashionable male style riding habit with a black bicorne decorated with bows and ostrich feathers. A long full trained skirt was draped over the horse. *c.*1680–1700.

LEFT: *c.*1642. Soldier wearing the popular buff coat with the 'lobster tail pot' helmet, cuirass back and front, and high bucket top boots.
CENTRE: Lady in a high waisted basqued bodice, slightly trained full skirt with a lace bertha and large lace cuffs. *c.*1645.
RIGHT: *c.*1670. Man wearing short wide breeches, open at the knees and loose fitting doublet.

or the front. When fastened in the front, from eyelet holes in the flaps attached to the bodice and by means of lacing, a stomacher was always present, this having a central rounded tab which sloped down in the centre front. Back fastening was from the high neckline to the waist being secured by lacing, hooks and eyes or, by the wealthier, with jewelled clasps; this back-fastening type was worn without a stomacher, although a mock one was sometimes worn. The high neckline at the back allowed for a very low décolletage in the front. When the bodice was worn without a basque, it was very close-fitting to the waist, coming to a point in the front which made it extremely stiff and uncomfortable. This style had both front and back fastening with girdle and sleeves in the same style for both types. The girdle was usually a narrow ribbon belt which followed the contours of the waistline.

Sleeves came in a variety of styles, but at this period, up to the 1640s they were full, often being ballooned and paned above and below the elbows, or were short and wide to the elbow with the full exposure of the chemise sleeve. The skirt, which was gathered loosely at the waist, fell in full folds to the ground, sometimes with a centre opening but the closed type skirt was becoming more popular, lasting into the 1650s. The fitted-bodice gown was joined to a full skirt and was often open down the front, this having great favour from 1625 to 1645. The older type of gown as an overgarment was sometimes incorporated into the newer fashions.

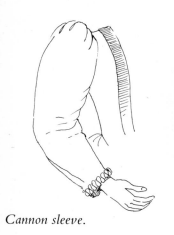

Cannon sleeve.

NECK AND WRISTWEAR
Ruffs and collars or bands were worn by the fashionable throughout the first half of the century and they came in all sizes and with a variety of names: *open, closed, cartwheel, oval, fan-shaped, standing and falling bands.*

Ruffs were worn with all types of necklines, high and low, apart from the fan-shaped ruff which was always worn with a low décolletage, the others could be worn with both. Among later styles of neckwear was the *bertha*, in fashion from 1625 to the 1650s, this surrounded the décolletage and met in the centre front and hung down in a narrow strip in front. A neckerchief was also worn around the shoulders and was sometimes fastened at the throat by a jewelled clasp. The *gorget,* which stayed in fashion until the 1660s, covered the whole décolletage like a cape, being fastened under the chin and the neck. The diaphanous *pinner* or *tucker* was used as a fill-in for the low décolletage.

For the first quarter of the century *hand ruffs* were very fashionable but were gradually superseded by the laced, turn-backed cuff attached to the bodice sleeves, or frills which were attached to the sleeves of the chemise.

CLOAKS

Cloaks were still popular for travelling and for cold and wet weather. Long to the ground they were secured at the neck by ties or cords with a centre-front closure of buttons. Cloaks were often lined with warm materials, including fur. The *tippet*, a cape which came to just below waist level, was a popular addition for warmth. Short loose coats which came to hip level as well as long overcoats with wide sleeves were also worn.

SHOES

Shoes were similar to men's, with heels and soles raised on cork though after about 1625 long skirts usually concealed the shoes. Boots were mainly worn for riding only. Legwear also resembled that of the men. *Chopines* and *pattens* (see Glossary) remained in use due to the poor condition of the roads. They became decorative and ornamental with scenes painted on them and some were even covered in fine leathers or silks, and worn more as a status symbol; for when they became really high, it was only possible to walk with them aided by the support of servants, therefore only the wealthier classes could afford them. The chopine was the forerunner of the heel, and the patten the predecessor of the platform sole. Chopines, originally a Venetian fashion, occasionally had indentations under the soles to give a heeled appearance. Pattens differed in that they were worn with separate shoes and held on by straps.

A double-soled shoe, popular from *c.*1630 had a similar effect of raising the heels, as did the chopine.

HEADWEAR

Although it was fashionable not to wear any head coverings, they were, to a limited extent, still worn. The *French hood,* with the back turned up over the front as a bongrace (see Glossary) gradually went out of fashion, being worn only by the elderly, gradually becoming smaller and worn further back, slightly peaked in the front.

Another fashion, the *Mary Stuart*, which had become quite popular towards the end of the sixteenth century, was a favourite in the early seventeenth century. This style was

Ladies shoe with rounded toe
and shoe rose, early seventeenth
century.

High cut shoe in brocade with
a falling lace collar, 1603–49.

Flat shoe with fastening under a
rosette, early seventeenth
century.

Silk slipper with large rosette
worn with a cork soled
pantoffle.

Double soled shoe with a long
and shaped toe piece and
decorated vamp, c.1695.

Double soles shoe in a striped
material with a thick wood or
cork sole decorated with a
rosette, early seventeenth
century.

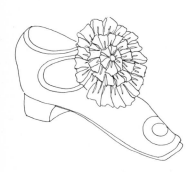

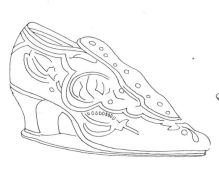

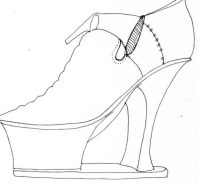

Square shaped shoe with a
large rose, early seventeenth
century.

Ladies double soled pantoffle
with a decorated vamp, early
seventeenth century.

Chopine-type shoe raised with
a double sole.

Square toed, silk bound leather shoe fastened with a matching silk bow, 1604–45.

Ladies soft leather shoe fastened over a wide strap with a buckle, the top is pleated and seamed, early seventeenth century.

usually of white lawn or lace with the wide border either stiffened with wire, or starched and lace trimmed. It was shaped to dip down the centre front with the sides standing out, close fitting on the head with a hanging piece at the back, adaptable to a bongrace. This remained in fashion with the older generation until the 1620s. A variation of this style, popular between 1620 and 1630, was an unstiffened type of cap made of a fine material curving round the front and straight at the back.

A long hood wired to form an arch over the forehead and extending over the face, similar to the late Elizabethan style, remained in fashion during the first half of the seventeenth century, still being worn for mourning and outdoor wear. It curved in at the neck or waistline, and was sometimes draped down to the ground, like a cape. Thin veils were worn by younger widows, and were cut or turned back and slightly stiffened so as to stand away from the head at the sides. After the middle of the century, they became softer and were draped with the front point forming a peak at the forehead. Shorter veils were also worn in the summer to protect the face from the sun.

The middle class and poorer people still wore *coifs*, similar to those of the sixteenth century, which were close-fitting caps made in one with a seam on the top. They were decorated with embroidery and usually had a string around the neck edge so that they could be fastened under the chin, thus alleviating the necessity for elaborate hairstyles, although the upper classes still wore them for informal wear, or beneath hats. A later style of coif, popular until about 1660, was shaped to fit over the hairstyle, with a band at the back. It was made in such a way that the seam was at the back with

Coronet headdress edged with
lace and embroidered, 1620–25.

Mary Stuart hat.

Muffler.

'Cavalier' style hat.

the extra material gathered at the crown with a drawstring
tying under the chin in the front. They were mainly of a
white material trimmed with lace.

Soft hoods had to accommodate the tall hairstyles and
were made of a double material with the front folded back
into a cuff shape framing the face and tied under the chin.
These were made in dark colours and were popular from the
1640s.

Hats, similar to Elizabethan styles were worn mainly for
riding and travelling, as the tall hairstyles made wearing
them difficult. A round-topped tall hat with a brim which
could be turned up on the side was much worn by the upper
classes and was embellished with plaited or twisted bands of
material as well as plumes and decorated with jewels.

Coif tilted over hairstyle.

Hairstyle consisting of a thin
curled fringe and loosely curled
side pieces, 1635–45.

High front hairstyle.

High crowned version of the
sugar loaf hat, popular during
the Commonwealth period,
c.1645.

Top hair brushed back with
partings either side. Bun at the
back decorated with jewellery
and ribbons.

Ladies beaver hat with a decorated hatband and standing band collar, c.1616.

Lady in 'golilla', a standing band collar, and a tall hat with an elaborate hatband and feather plume, c.1616.

Country women and the middle classes wore hats over coifs made of linen with the hair just raised over the forehead.

After the first quarter of the seventeenth century a lower crowned hat with a wide brim in a variety of styles, either flat, wavy or turned up, was fashionable for riding and was worn with a hatband and ostrich feathers. This was known as the *Cavalier* style. The middle classes wore a variation known as a *Sugar Loaf* hat with a flat-topped crown and hatband which could be plaited. These kinds of hats were usually made of either beaver or felt, and were popular up to the Restoration period.

HAIRSTYLES

The tall hairstyles, so popular in the latter part of Queen Elizabeth's reign, continued so during the first part of James I's reign.

Hair was high at the front, being placed over pads or

curved wire frames, whilst the back was in a flat bun around which, occasionally, were thin plaits. If no bun was worn, all the hair was arranged over the front to give more thickness and height. Single hair ornaments were very popular and *cauls* and *nets* were still worn with the edging of precious stones or metals. Ribbon *bows* and *plumes* were also worn by fashionable ladies. After about 1608 hair was not worn so high and by about 1614 the tall wire frames were superseded by pads only. Hair was not brushed as high, but back from the forehead with the sides fluffed out; back hair, however, was still placed in a bun whilst side hair was cut short to just below the ears. Replacing the jewelled ornamentation were ribbon bows and feathers – quite short and in bunches.

With the advent of Charles I in 1625 hairstyles began to alter, there now being a parting either side, with the sides hanging in ringlets, and the centre part pulled back with the rest of the back hair formed into a flat bun. The fringe still remained fashionable, but was gradually replaced by small curls over the forehead, these becoming fewer, until only a long ringlet at the sides remained. The back hair was then braided in a circle entwined with pearls or ribbons tied with bows. Oval-shaped pearls were popularly worn as earrings and occasionally as hair ornamentation. Hats were not fashionable during the Stuart period, lace-edged caps and hoods being more popular to protect the elaborate hairstyles.

Until about 1625 the Elizabethan styles remained, the front hair being brushed high over rolls or wire supports, the back hair being coiled into a flat bun. Ornamentation was by way of pins and jewels shaped into stars, crescents and arrows. False hair and wigs were still worn.

After 1620 a small fringe and frizzed hair at the sides with curls hanging over the ears and a flat bun at the back became the mode with hair, thereafter becoming longer with formal curls massed at the sides; fringes became longer and were formed into flat curls; hair became flatter on top and plaited or coiled into a bun which was decorated with pearls or drooping feathers at the back.

In the 1640s the side curls became longer and were formed into ringlets. A parting each side of the head just above the ears allowed the rest of the hair to be combed straight back, the bun at the back becoming larger and decorated with ribbon bows, jewels, feathers or a small caul. Pearls could also be entwined in the bun.

Puritan ladies had short straight hair brushed back, or with a centre parting. A high crowned hat was often worn

Fringed hairstyle, 1620–35.

Hair brushed back and braided with loose side curled pieces, 1654–1660.

Brushed back style headdress, 1615–25.

The lady above is wearing a winter style dress with chaperon, fur stole collar and hand muff. For face protection she wore a half face mask, c.1644.

over a close-fitting white cap.

Cavalier ladies, however, had long hair with masses of curls and ringlets to the shoulders with ribbon bows and jewels entwined in the hair.

Just before the Restoration of Charles II (1660), hairstyles became shorter, to just below ear level with waves at the sides.

ACCESSORIES

Aprons were worn as ornamentation at home by the fashionable ladies. They were usually of a fine transparent material with lace trimmings, whilst plain white aprons were usually worn by the working classes.

Gloves and *handkerchiefs* were similar to those used by the men.

Muffs, like the men's, were not large at the beginning of the century, but reached their largest in the 1640s, after which they again became smaller. They were worn either suspended around the neck by a cord, or carried in the hand.

Mufflers, or *chin clouts,* popular until the 1660s, were worn for warmth, as were short scarves.

Masks, first popular in the late Elizabethan era, remained fashionable throughout the century. Full masks covering the entire face, made of velvet, satin or silk, were worn as a protection against inclement weather, as well as a disguise. These were known as 'vizards' and held in place with a bead which was fastened inside the mask and held between the teeth. Half-masks, which were also worn were tied at the back of the head. The *loo mask,* a half mask favoured by fashionable men and women was worn as protection as well as for coquetry out-of-doors. Ornate fans were also used for the same purposes.

Lady's face patches.

Perfume was used in great quantities, on both clothes and gloves which were nearly always scented with jasmine and other fragrances.

Cosmetics were much used in the Stuart period, especially white chalk for powder and rouge. Cosmetics remained similar to those of the previous century, with lip dyes and rouge, and the use of ceruse powder (white lead). 'Spanish leather', which was dyed scarlet, was often used to colour the skin. 'Plumpers', made of cork, were placed inside the mouth on either side to fill out the cheeks. False eyebrows were sometimes worn and were made of mouse skin. Face patches in the shapes of circles, crescent moons and stars were worn, sometimes as many as 15 at once. These were often worn to hide the blemishes on the face.

Roundheads and Restoration:

Commonwealth (1649–60); Charles II (1660–85); James II (1685–89); William and Mary (1689–1702)

Men

DOUBLET

With a few variations the short, close fitting doublet with the narrow skirt, continued in fashion until the 1670s. The strange method of buttoning halfway down the chest, leaving the lower part open, made a large gap between the doublet and the breeches which was bridged by revealing the shirt which protruded through. The neckline of the doublet remained high standing and rigid, being stiffened with buckram. The sleeves with the open top seam finished at the elbow, and the turned-back cuffs were trimmed with loops of ribbon. Other forms of sleeves had no open seams and ended at the elbow with turned-back cuffs fastened with buttons. After the 1660s, the doublet began to be replaced by the coat and waistcoat.

COAT

In the late 1660s, the terms used today: jacket, waistcoat, coat, became the general names used for male dress. The first coats were made to fit the shoulders only; they did not fit the figure (nor was there a discernable waistline) but hung loosely down to just below the knees. Long coat-skirts were divided into back and side vents which came up to hip level. The neckline was plain and without a collar. The coat was closed down the centre front, from the neckline to the hem, with a close row of buttons, but similar to the earlier gown; it was more often than not left open to reveal the waistcoat.

Pockets were large openings cut in a horizontal or vertical position, low on the coat and buttoned to prevent them sagging open.

Gentlemen, c.1634. The man
on the left wears a waistcoat
of the petticoat variety with a
flared shirt; pockets cut
horizontally and cuffs
buttoned. The hat is trimmed
with ribbon loops to match the
waistcoat.

On the right one can see the
more fashionable style of open
coat without waistcoat. Knee
breeches are worn over rolled-up
stockings. He is also wearing
a Steinkirk cravat.

The Puritan style male dress
in sombre colours consisted of a
sugar loaf hat in felt and
beaver, cossack style coats
buttoned or laced with a bib
style collar, c.1649.

The woman wore a hitched up
overskirt which was secured
at the back. The collar was in
the deep neckerchief style, and
for headwear she wore a linen
coif or bonnet, c.1649.

*Long leather buff coat and
helmet and cuirass worn by
James II.*

Sleeves followed the doublet fashion, short to the elbow
and finishing in a deep cuff which was fastened to the sleeves
by a top button, whilst it remained open behind. The vent
decoration was trimmed with sham button-holes and buttons.

By the late 1680s and the early 1690s, a further change took
place. The coat now became closer fitting with a slight waist-
ing whilst the length stayed just below the knee. The sleeves
became longer and finished almost at the wrist and ended
in a turn-back cuff.

The extreme fashion of wearing a bunch of looped ribbons, called *shoulder knots*, on the right shoulder was merely the forerunner of a later profusion of ribbon bows and loops on male clothes. By the 1690s fashionable men wore tailor-fitted clothes which clearly defined the waistline. Skirts were fuller and fanned out from the pleats sewn on the side vents. The length remained unchanged to just below the knee and the coat stayed collarless. The front fastening remained unchanged though it was seldom used as fashion did not allow for gentlemen, regardless of the weather, to fasten their coats. Pockets however had changed their position to just under the waistline.

WAISTCOAT

After the late 1660s, the waistcoat followed the cut and pattern of the coat with a few minor differences. The sleeves were closer fitting and longer; the habit of turning the waistcoat sleeve cuff over the coat cuff was very fashionable. As sometimes the waistcoat was hidden by the coat, the back pieces were often made of inferior material referred to rather appropriately as 'cheats'. Some waistcoats were worn without the coat and from 1690 they were cut to finish just below the knee.

OUTER-GARMENTS

Overcoats as outer-garments were both long and short. The *Brandenburg,* named after the Prussian city famous for wool, was similar to the loose-fitting winter coat called the *cassock*. The *jump jacket* was a winter thigh-length coat fastened down the front with a vent up the back.

CLOAK

By the late 1670s the cloak was no longer a fashionable item and its functional usage was that of a utility article of clothing. After hundreds of years of being in and out of fashion, its main purpose was taken over by the overcoat.

NECK AND WRISTWEAR

The deep turned-down collar with the edge to edge meeting in the front was the popular falling band type to the 1670s. The neckcloth, later called the *cravat*, was popular in the late 1660s and remained in fashion into the next century. With short coat sleeves in fashion, the shirt sleeve cuffs were adorned with a variety of frills and ruffles.

The gentleman on the left
wore petticoat breeches which
were trimmed with ribbon loops.
The doublet was short, and he
wore a falling band collar and
large cannons, c.1660.
The lady on the right wore a
gown with a trained skirt and
close fitting bodice with a
stomacher. The sleeves were
short revealing the short deep
frilled chemise sleeve. Round
the neck was worn the steinkirk
cravat, and the headdress was
in the fontange style, c.1693.
The gentlemen on the far right
wore the fashionable open coat
with a waistcoat. The breeches
were worn with rolled up
stockings fastened below the
knee. The cocked hat had a
feather decoration, c.1693

Until the late 1670s, the open breeches, similar to modern shorts, were very popular and decorated on the lower side seams with bunches of ribbon loops. The bizarre taste for *Rhinegrave pantaloons*, known also as *petticoat breeches*, in the late 1670s was without doubt the strangest of all fashions. The breeches were extremely wide and fell below the knee attached in pleats to a waistband. Because of their fullness, they were often mistaken for a divided skirt. In addition, the loose lining was allowed to hang down below the breeches, giving a greater illusion of a petticoat, and following the trend, were also lavishly decorated with ribbon loops.

Worn also were the *closed breeches* which were full at the seat and fell to overhang the knee or could be turned up into a cuff effect. In the last decade of the century, closer-fitting plain breeches without any decoration were worn.

Leather vest, c.1680. This had a central fastening down the front from the neckline to waist level with a double row of brass buttons and buttonholes. The flapped pockets with a buttonhole at each end were at waist level.

The large loose coat, called a
Brandenburg reached to calf
length and was buttoned with
cord made from wool. The
waistcoat was long to the knees,
the cocked hat trimmed with
feathers and ribbon loops,
c.1674.

STOCKINGS

From the Restoration the words 'hose' and 'stocking' became interchangeable, with hose no longer being used to mean breeches. Hose were made of knitted silk for the fashionable, knitted wool for the middle classes and in a tailored material for everyday wear.

They were held up by sash garters until about 1680, made of ribbon loops and tied on the outside below the knees, then plain ones, which were strips of material fastened with a buckle, over which the stockings could be rolled.

Boot hose, with ornamental tops continued in favour until the 1680s. Stirrup hose, also very fashionable until that date, had wide tops which could be attached to the petticoat breeches with which they were invariably worn.

Cannons, not to be confused with canions (see illustration on page 9 and page 16), were ornamental extensions to the stockings when worn with either petticoat or open breeches. They were often in a material similar to the coat.

SHOES

Shoes did not alter very much, with the exception of higher backs or quarters. Toes were still flat and square and buckles were still popular, often being square, corresponding to the shape of toe. Heels gradually became extremely high. Most heels, however, were curved and, due to their incorrect positioning, the shoe was steeply angled.

Red heels became more popular, although they could be coloured in other shades.

Boots became more close-fitting, except those worn by the Cavaliers, which were extravagant in both shape and designs.

Roundheads wore a great deal of leather; their armour could be leather as well as the ammunition bags, drinking bottles and belts, etc.

As the toes became less squared, cuffs were replaced by tall tabs and shoes were not so high. They were fastened by a metal or jewelled buckle on the tab, which could be turned back to reveal a contrasting colour.

Perfumed sachets were sometimes placed in the folds of Cavaliers' boots.

Shoes worn by the Puritans were plain and square toed with a small heel. The tab in front stood high and could be decorated with a metal buckle or sometimes a strap threaded through and fastened with a buckle on the outside.

The *postillion boot* was usually of a thick black leather. The

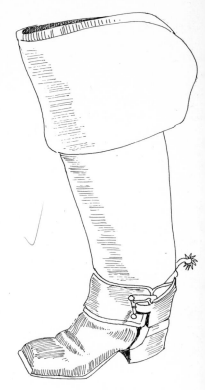

Jack boot of stiff black leather with several layers of leather for the heels, they had bucket tops and square toes and were worn with spurs, c.1660.

High tongued shoe fastened under a small rosette.

Buff leather boot with triple lace at the top. Square toed with square stirrup leather secured to the straps with leather knots, first part of seventeenth century.

Stirrup guard plaque worn over a boot with boot hose worn inside.

French style boot hose, usually worn with red heels, first half of seventeenth century.

Gentlemans high tongued shoe with a ribbon knot and fastened with a buckle, c.1660.

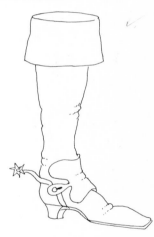

Boot with cup shaped top and stirrup guard, c.1627.

Medium tongued shoe, c.1690.

spurs were attached by leather links to a decorated and appliquéd bootguard. The knee-guard, which was separate, was fitted over the top.

With the return of Charles II from France in 1660, shoe fashions were again changed. The Louis heel, with its curved front and the more delicate shapes, made shoes an important feature of fashion. Soles were sometimes slotted and could carry letters inside them.

After the 1660s red heels and red-edged soles were worn only on fashionable occasions. Shoes had squared toes and high square heels with open sides, popular in the first half of the century, becoming more closed, until by 1680 they were

The merchant and his wife on
the left wore the dress typical
of the Commonwealth period,
c.1650.

The farm labourer wore the
short jerkin and breeches with
coarse stockings, c.1650.

Fireman's bucket used in the
Fire of London, c.1666.

Fireman's leather helmet as
worn in the Fire of London,
c.1666.

completely closed. Tongues were high and squared from
1680–1720 and after 1690 they were turned down to reveal
a red lining.

Straps from the heel leathers fastened over the tongues
with ribbons and rosettes until 1660, after which date,
(until about 1680) ornamental ribbon bows were used.

Buckles were used as a form of fastening from the 1660s,
being small and oval until the 1680s, when they became more
square shaped until about 1710.

Boots became less fashionable for ordinary wear after the
Restoration and were only worn for riding. They still had
deep turned down cuffs (extremely ornate and sometimes
edged with bands of lace which matched the lace on the
clothes) which could hide perfume sachets.

The tops of boots were generally light in colour, tan being
popular whilst the rest of the boots were black.

Heavy *jackboots* made of stiff leather were fairly close
fitting, laced on the outer edge, with the tops turned down
below knee level. Lighter jackboots, worn from about
1675, were of a softer leather and fitted by lacing or button
either down the front or on the outer side.

Spatterdashes, worn from the 1670s, were leggings shaped
like long fitted boots and were worn with shoes. Where
they met the shoe, large spur leathers were worn, thus covering the join to give the appearance of boots.

Buckles of all shapes and sizes were becoming quite usual,
as were shoe laces, which were worn by both males and
females.

Shoes and stockings took the place of tall boots except
for horse riding and the vamps (see Glossary) became

Puritan felt hat with a narrow hatband and a small buckle in the front, 1620s.

Puritan beaver hat with a silk band and large buckle, 1630s.

longer and narrower, with the toes squared. The tabs, which were high, sometimes folded forward to reveal coloured lining.

As stage coaches became more popular after *c.*1640, the need for protective shoes became less, although for ordinary street wear, protection was still required. This usually took the form of pattens edged in metal.

'Jacked' (stiff) leather was waxed and coated with tar and pitch to make it waterproof. This was the origin of 'jack boots', and also the beginning of patent leather.

Inside boots was sometimes worn a small shoe or slipper to protect the feet.

Mules made of Morocco leather were worn by men and women, women also wearing *pantoffles* of satin in various pale shades, which had high heels and decorative tabs.

Large rosettes, sometimes with a jewel in the centre, continued to be very fashionable.

Leather heels were not so popular at this time, although heels were covered in either leather or fabric.

From 1682–1714 shoes were mainly of black leather with red heels which became higher. Shoe buckles were beginning to replace the rosettes and bows and were very ornamental.

HEADWEAR
From the 1640s to the 1670s, the *Sugar Loaf* hat was worn, similar to the *Capotain* worn in the first half of the century.

LEFT: *c.*1660. Petticoat breeches with multiple ribbon loops and a short doublet, sugar loaf hat and shoes with large bows.

CENTRE: *c.*1668. Close fitting boned bodice coming to a deep point in front with a low décolletage covered by a transparent shawl, sleeves full to the elbow, revealing the full, frilled sleeves of the chemise, the full skirt hung in folds to the ground open in front.

RIGHT: *c.*1672. Boy wearing the fashion of the adults with short-sleeved type of smock.

TOP: *c.*1693. Tight-fitting bodice, low décolletage and elbow-length sleeves with deep frilled cuffs. The trained skirt was pulled back and fixed with a bow, revealing the underskirt. A fontange headdress was also worn.

TOP LEFT: Horse Grenadier with the
uniform in the same style and fashion
as civilian wear. *c.*1690.
CENTRE: Man wearing slightly waisted
coat and waistcoat profusely
decorated with buttons and braid,
full breeches and wig. *c.*1690.
RIGHT: Man wearing a jerkin with
wings and sham hanging sleeves with
the cloak bag breeches fashion, and
soft high leather boots. *c.*1625.

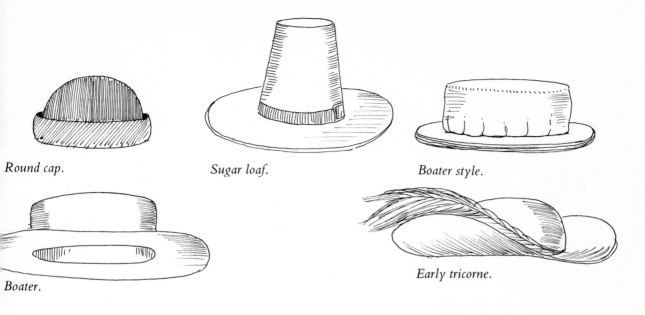

Round cap.

Sugar loaf.

Boater style.

Boater.

Early tricorne.

High crown.

It had a cone-shaped crown with a rounded or flat top. The brim could be adorned with feathers or ribbons.

A wide-brimmed boater-shaped hat, also trimmed with feathers or ribbons, became popular from between 1665 and 1675.

A low-crowned hat, with a broad brim which could be cocked in various positions and known as the *Monmouth Cock*, was decorated with plumes or ribbons up until the 1680s, but from about 1675 could also be embellished with braid.

In the last decade of the century the *Tricorne* was fashionable. The brim was cocked in equal proportions, forming a triangle with a point in the front and decorated with ostrich-feather tips around a brim edged with braid.

A round-crowned cap with a closely turned up flat brim, divided front and back and could be covered with fur, was worn informally or for sport as well as for warmth indoors.

Nightcaps were worn indoors when wigs were removed, as usually the head had been shaved.

WIGS

Wigs did not become popular wear until Charles II's reign (1660–85) and then were worn only by the upper classes. Besides real hair, they were also made of goat's and horse hair. On earlier wigs, the hair had been sewn on a close-fitting silk cap, but later, when wig making became an

Large French style wig worn with a Steinkirk cravat, c.1695–1700.

important art, the strands were individually threaded through a canvas and knotted and by about 1665, the upper classes wore them to a great extent in blond, brown or black. As these wigs were uncomfortable to wear, hair was either cut very short or shaved off and indoors a nightcap or skull cap was worn instead.

The first wigs had a centre parting, with the hair hanging down in curls, but by the 1670s they were more elaborate and artificial in appearance.

Wig fashions varied; some were a cascade of curls, later ones became smaller and resembled more natural-looking hair, whilst the largest with their formal curls were known as *periwigs*.

The *full-bottomed* wig in this period consisted of neat ringlets which hung down over the shoulders and down the back and men's wigs began to copy the ladies' hairstyles of tall headdress with curls over the forehead, raised each side like horns.

The *Campaign wig*, worn from about 1675, was a full wig, but shorter than the full-bottomed. It had one or two corkscrew curls with a queue (a short 'tail') at the back and was worn mainly by soldiers or during recreation.

During the 1670s the hair had become so cumbersome that many men had begun to tie the hair back at the nape of the neck.

After Charles I's execution (1649) and until the 1680s beards were considered unfashionable, but very thin moustaches remained in vogue. Wigs became so large that the wearing of hats became unpopular and by the 1690s periwigs became so enormous that they were divided into three portions, one either side hanging over the shoulders and the third part at the back. They could have hair as long as waist level, the left side sometimes being longer than the right.

By the end of the seventeenth century, light brown or grey scented powder was used on wigs with curls being formed on heated clay rollers around which the hair was tightly wound. It is interesting to note that it was also fashionable to comb one's hair in public.

ACCESSORIES

Gauntlet gloves were still worn in the second half of the century, as well as longer gloves which reached to the elbow.

Decorated *handkerchiefs* were still fashionable until about 1670.

Large *muffs*, made in a variety of materials such as furs, satins and velvets, decorated with ribbon loops and lined in a contrasting material, were worn suspended from the neck or could be attached to a waist belt or coat button.

Fashionable young gentlemen carried long canes as well as mirrors, combs and snuff boxes, although jewellery was less popular.

Snuff boxes became very popular and the designs on these silver or porcelain boxes were often repeated on shoe decorations.

Gentlemen often wore earrings, face patches and even make-up. Moustache bands of Spanish origin and beard boxes were worn at night to preserve the shapes.

Women

BODICE

Continuing in fashion was the separate body and skirt up to the 1680s. The bodice was very close fitting, heavily boned and, as in earlier fashions, long waisted, dipping to a deep point in the front. The neck was low and well off the shoulders being edged with a chemise frill. A *bertha* of lace covered the low décolletage. The bodice was closed either at the front or the back by lacing and sometimes the shoulder seams were open, and closed with lacing.

The *stomacher* continued in fashion as a cover for the tight lacing of the bodice, it was very decorative and the fashion for *echelles*, rows of ribbon bows arranged in line, was a most elegant style. Sleeves varied and some were full to the elbow from which the chemise sleeve issued. Often the bodice

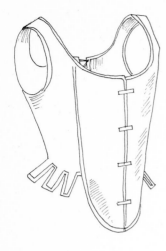

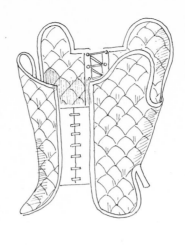

Bodice waistcoat with stiffened
front, the back being laced,
c.1670.

Quilted bodice with back lacing,
and hooks and eye fastening at
the front, c.1670.

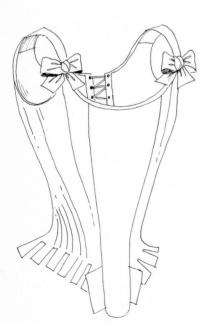

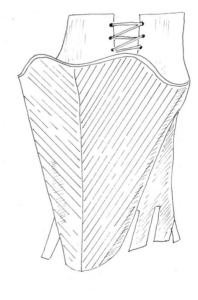

Bodice with cane or whalebone
stiffening, c.1660.

Cane stiffened corset with back
lacing, c.1625.

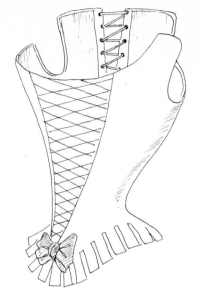
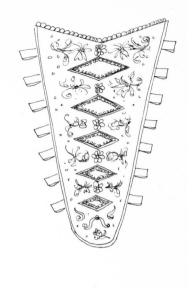

Whalebone stiffened corset with back lacing and a false front, c.1660.

Embroidered stomacher with linen tabs for securing to the bodice, c.1660–70.

sleeve had a top-seam opening through which the chemise sleeve emerged. Another variation was the wide sleeve which ended at the elbow and was lined with a lace fall and chemise sleeve exposed to the wrist. A short plain sleeve which finished at the elbow followed the male fashion with a trimming of ribbon loops as decoration.

SKIRT
In this later period the skirt was pleated to the waist and allowed to fall to the ground in loose irregular folds with an inverted V-shape opening at the front revealing the decorative underskirt. The edges of the overskirt were arranged in a variety of ways – pulled or turned back and fastened by clasps. About mid-century the skirts became trained and by the 1680s were extremely long and very fashionable. During the same period, the *Cul-de-Paris,* an early type of bustle, made its first appearance, with the train of the skirt pulled up behind to give bustle effect style still more pronounced.

GOWN
In the early 1680s the joined bodice and skirt came into fashion. The bodice was fairly close fitting and was attached to a full trained skirt, often hitched up, with a centre front

opening to reveal the underskirt. The bodice fitted round the back of the neck, over the shoulders, and meeting in a V shape at the waist, the space between being filled in by an embroidered stomacher. The sleeves were usually short to the elbow and ending in a turned-up cuff. By the 1690s lace frills were attached to the cuffs of the sleeves in place of the chemise-frilled sleeve.

PETTICOAT
Similar in cut to the skirt, the petticoat was also slightly trained but made a little shorter to just above ankle length. The petticoat was very decorative and was trimmed with lace flounces at the hem, or at hip level.

NECKWEAR
The *Steinkirk cravat* was a male military fashion taken up by the ladies. It was a wide lawn scarf wrapped round the neck, the ends being twisted together in front, then pinned to the left side of the bodice. Also worn was the *gorget*, an earlier fashion, which, after the late 1670s became old fashioned. The *whisk*, similar to the gorget, continued to be worn in the 1690s. Sleeves often matched the neckwear.

COATS
Coats, usually loose fitting, followed the male fashion, worn by ladies in bad weather and for horse riding. From the 1680s the *tippet* became very fashionable; it fell to waist length and the upper small cape became a deep collar. The *Pallatine* was in reality a sable tippet style.

SHOES
It wasn't until the Restoration that shoe fashions changed noticeably. They became more pointed with high Louis heels and were fastened with buckled straps. Shoes were made in a variety of materials from leather to brocades and silks which were often embroidered for fashionable occasions. Long buskins, or boots, usually made of leather, were worn for riding.

Boudoir slippers could even have a lace cuff around the ankle and were frequently embroidered also.

Ladies shoes, to make them more dainty, often had spatula shaped toes.

Stockings were nearly always knitted and in a great variety of colours.

Ladies shoe made of a material, bound in a contrasting colour to match the bow. The almost wedge shaped heel was also covered in material, 1649–60.

Ladies leather riding boot with a close fitting front and elastic gusset, second part of the seventeenth century.

Silk shoe with embroidered front and small tongue, c.1660.

Leather shoe with apliquéd braid, the toe extended over the sole of the shoe c.1660–80.

Plain silk shoe, 1660–80.

Pantoffle.

Quilted satin mule with a taffeta frill at the top. The thick heel also was covered in fabric and the toe was shallow and square, 1660–68.

Mule.

Shoe with tapered toe, the heel so placed as to give the shoe a steep forward tilt, late seventeenth century.

Embroidered brocade shoe with the high heel silk covered and so placed as to give the shoe a sharp forward angle. The tapered toe often projected over the sole, mid-seventeenth century.

Embroidered silk mule with a plain silk collar band and covered heel.

HEADWEAR

Built-up hair continued in fashion in the 1690s reaching extreme heights by the end of the century with the addition of the *fontange* headdress (see Glossary). The fontange headdress was basically a small linen cap worn on the back of the head with tall, pleated and stiffened tiers of linen or lace placed in front and either set narrower towards the top or fanned outwards. These tiers were supported by a wire frame called a 'commode'. Two long lappets hung behind the cap made of the same material and, occasionally, pinned up to the crown at the sides. Sometimes this type of headdress was ornamented with ribbon knots. Coloured or black silk hoods, taller than previously, were draped over the cap of the fontange for outdoor wear and were tied in front.

Country women wore straw hats over coifs or hoods with brims, of differing widths, often pulled down at the sides and fastened with ribbons tied under the chin.

Large tall crowned hats were worn by the middle classes between 1650–70, although it was quite usual to go bareheaded.

Chaperons, which were a type of soft hood, tied under the chin, were most popular from *c.*1640 until the end of the century.

The *cornet,* a linen, lace-edged cap or coif, fitted the back of the head with lappets or streamers down each side of the face.

Fontange headdress built up with heavy lace and secured with ribbon bows, c.1690

Chaperon, c.1642.

In the 1660s hairstyles became much wider with a centre parting and the hair placed over wire frames on each side. False curls were added to give a puffed out effect. By the Restoration hair was parted in the centre with less width, and ringlets became popular.

For about ten years after the Restoration the side hair was wired to give width to the ringlets which hung down with the front hair brushed back and placed in a bun at the back. After this period the wiring of curls away from the cheeks became less fashionable and the ringlets were allowed to fall over the shoulders, with an odd curl over the forehead.

A hairstyle, first fashionable in Paris, known as the *Hurluberlu*, consisted of masses of close curls in rows over the head, whilst the back hair was in a bun with ringlets falling over the shoulders and the nape of the neck.

Centre partings with curls at the sides became popular in the 1680s and hairstyles generally became higher again in the front, with false hair being added where necessary. Small hair ornamentations were used a great deal on the front hair.

After 1690 the front of the hair became higher, sometimes in peaks, either side of the parting. It was achieved with the aid of padded rolls and a wire known as 'palisade'. This tall hairstyle was called a *Tour* and was often decorated with ribbon knots with the top-knot a large bow. The hair then fell in either loose hanging ringlets or was pinned up. Curls were known as 'confidants' by the ears, 'favourites' either side of the forehead, whilst those at the nape of the neck were called 'crêve-coeurs'. They were achieved by the use of curling irons or curl papers and were set with gum arabic. False hair was also much used.

Jewelled pins, called *firmaments* were also worn as decoration.

Children

Children still dressed in imitation of their elders and even the elaborate hairstyles were very similar. Lace or embroidered bonnets were worn by boys to the age of about five, and by girls up to about ten. The boys' hair was shoulder length, either straight or in ringlets with a fringe combed to one side. With the more elaborate hairstyles of the 1660s small curls made their appearance on the forehead and side ringlets were almost shoulder length.

Dutch type hairstyle with
wired stand away curls,
c.1660.

Hairstyle built up over a
palisade, c.1690.

Hairstyle with centre parting,
c.1680.

Ringlet hairstyle, c.1675.

Wired hairstyle, c.1665.

Short embroidered wrist *gloves*, often ornamented with lace or ribbon loops were worn. Long close-fitting elbow length gloves were worn on formal occasions. They were usually made of silk or a soft leather. The use of scent on gloves continued and was still fashionable. For summer, long plain silk or lace *mittens* were popular for outdoor wear, whilst shorter silk mittens which could be embroidered, and were slit at the top to fit more snugly were also very fashionable.

Ornamented and tasselled *handkerchiefs* were less popular after the Restoration. Plain lawn or linen edged with lace becoming more fashionable.

Muffs, which had become smaller, were still used, and fur scarves were long and twisted around the neck in winter for warmth.

Large *fans,* some of which could be painted and perfumed, were popular and had decorative handles. They were made to fold up. Others could be made of feathers.

Long canes were also carried.

Laced tippet.

Sable fur Pallatine.

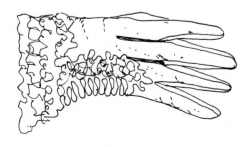

Wrist gloves.

Gentleman of high fashion with muff, c.1693.

Glossary

Baldrick	Belt worn diagonally across the chest, used for suspending swords etc. Sometimes also known as a 'shoulder belt'.
Banjan	Short-skirted knee-length coat, mainly worn indoors.
Basque	Short skirt-like extension of a bodice from the waistline.
Belly-piece	Stiff triangular piece of either pasteboard or buckram and whalebone in the lining of a doublet to fill in the front. Similar to a rigid corset.
Bob Wig	Undress wig without a queue.
Bombast	Padding such as horsehair, wool or cotton, used to puff out garments.
Bongrace	Front projection of a headdress.
Boot Hose	Coarse stockings worn over finer ones as protection.
Brandenburg	Long loose winter overcoat, usually cord trimmed and fastened with frogging.
Buff Coat	Military type of leather jerkin made of strong leather. Sleeves, if any, could be made of material.
Bum Roll	Padded roll worn for widening the hips.
Buskins	Knee-high leather boots.
Campaign Wig	Bushy wig with short curls at the sides and a short queue at the back.
Canions	Extensions of trunk hose, often in a contrasting colour.
Cannons	Decorative frills on the top of stockings, worn only with petticoat breeches or open breeches, and folded over the garters, forming flounces at the knees.
Cassock	Long loose overcoat, buttoning down the front, with sometimes a cape collar.
Caul	Net foundation upon which wigs were built in the late seventeenth and eighteenth centuries. A trellised skull cap in the sixteenth and seventeenth century.
Chaperone	Small soft hood worn on informal occasions.

Chemise	Undergarment.
Chin Clouts	Diagonally folded square of material worn over mouth and chin like a muffler for protection against the cold.
Chopines	Wooden overshoes built high with a cork or wooden sole.
Cod Piece	Front fastening of breeches, previously a pouch at the fork.
Coif	Under cap.
Commode	Wire frame to hold lace or frills upright on the fontange headdress.
Confidantes	Small curls by the ears.
Copotain	Conical crowned hat with the sides of the brim rolled.
Cravat	Neckerchief of a fine material worn around the neck with the ends either tied in a knot or bow.
Crêve-Coeur	Locks or curls at the nape of the neck.
Cul-de-Paris	Kind of bustle, the skirt at the back pulled up in order to stand out.
Décolletage	Low neckline.
Doublet	Padded jacket worn over shirt, close fitting and waisted.

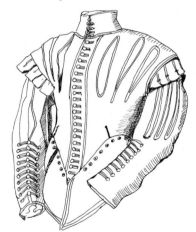

Dutch Cloak	Wide sleeved short cloak decorated extravagantly.
Echelles	Stomacher trimmed down the front with ribbon bows, one above the other.
Engageants	Deep double frills or ruffles.
Farthingale	Structure of shaped hoops of either whalebone, wire or wood, used to distend skirts.
Favourites	Curls on the forehead.
Fontange	Small flat crowned linen cap with a lace erection in the front with pendants hanging behind.
French Hood	Small bonnet type hood made on a stiffened frame.
Full Bottomed Wig	Large wig with centre parting, curls framing the face and hanging to shoulder length.

Galligaskins	Knee breeches.
Gamaches	Long cloth leggings worn as protection against dirt.
Garters	Narrow bands tied either above or below knee level to hold up stockings.
Girdlestead	Waistline.
Gorget	Small crescent shaped piece of metal suspended round the neck by a chain for men. For ladies it was a square deep cape-like collar.
Hanging Sleeves	Long wide tubular sleeves with a slit in the upper half through which the arm could protrude, leaving the rest of the sleeve hanging. These could reach extreme lengths. The sham hanging sleeves were streamers attached to the back of the armholes.

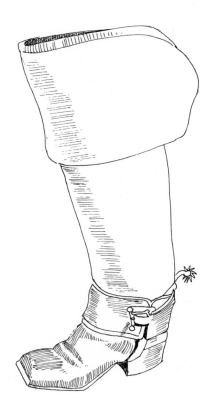

Jack Boots	Boots made of hard wearing leather, hardened by boiling or being painted with pitch. The tops were expanded bucket tops with the backs scooped out to allow for the bending of knees. Fastening was by lacing or buttoning on the outside.
Louis Heel	Heel with the sole continuing up the arch and down the front of the heel.
Lovelock	Curled lock of hair falling over the chest from the nape of the neck.

Mandilion	Loose hip length jacket with open sides.
Mantua	Loose unboned bodice with trained gown, the front, open to reveal the decorative underskirt.
Monmouth Cap	Knitted tall crowned brimless cap, made mainly in Wales.

Mouche	Small black patch worn as adornment on the face.
Muckinder	Handkerchief.
Mule	Type of slipper without the heel piece or quarter.
Nightgown	Long loose gown worn indoors for informal occasions.
Palisade	Wire frame supporting a fontange headdress, like a commode.
Pallatine	Sable fur shoulder wrap with ends hanging down the front.

65

Panes	Parallel slashings in material, or narrow strips of material joined at each end giving the appearance of slashings.
Pantoffles	Overshoes, similar to mules.
Partlet	Sleeveless jacket, like a fill-in for a low décolletage.
Pattens	Wooden overshoes raised on iron rings.
Peascod	Padding in front at waist level to give a protruding bulge over the girdle of a doublet.
Periwig	Wig, false hair covering.
Pinner	Fill-in for a low décolletage. Streamers of headwear pinned up, or a plain cap worn indoors.
Plumpers	Thin round cork balls put in the mouth to fill out the cavity of hollow cheeks.
Points	Ties for attaching, or used decoratively in bunches of ribbon bows.
Pumps	Soft flat heeled shoes with thin soles.
Queue	Hanging tail of a wig.
Quarters	Top back part of the shoe covering the heel to the vamp.
Rabato	Starched or wired support for a ruff.
Rever	Turned back edge of a garment, like a modern lapel.
Rhinegraves	or petticoat breeches. Like a divided skirt, full and gathered at the waist, falling to just above knee level. Trimmed with ribbon loops at the waist and outer side of the legs.
Ruff	Circular collar, gathered at the neck.

Scallops	Decorative edging with rounded indentations.
Slops	Short breeches ending loosely above the knees.
Spanish Cloak	Short cloak with a hood.
Spanish Hose	High waisted breeches pleated to a waistband, the legs narrowing down to the knees. Fastened on the outer side with ten to twelve buttons.
Spatterdashes	Leggings of a strong material or leather, fastened with either lacing, buttons or buckles on the outside.
Startups	High above-ankle shoes, either buckled or laced, worn mainly by country people.
Steinkirk	Long lace edged cravat knotted beneath the chin. The ends could be passed through a buttonhole or pinned to the coat. So called after the Battle of Steinkirk in 1692.
Stirrup Hose	Long overstockings without soles, but with a strap under the foot to hold them down.

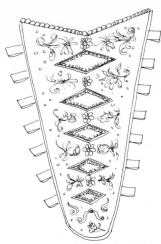

Stomacher	Ornamental panel filling the gap at the front of a low décolletage.
Sugarloaf Hat	Hat with a high conical crown and a broad rolled brim at the sides.
Tippet	Hanging streamers.
Tour	False curls added to front hair.
Tricorne	Hat with the brim turned back to form three points.
Trunk	or cannon sleeves. Fairly wide sleeves at the top, narrowing to the wrist.
Vamp	Upper front part of a shoe or boot.

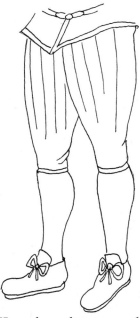

Venetians	Knee breeches, pear shaped with bombast around the hips.
Vizard	Whole complete mask.
Whisk	Broad lace trimmed falling collar, similar to a gorget.
Wings	Mainly crescent shaped projections on shoulder seams.

Bibliography

Arnold, J., *A Handbook of Costume*, Macmillan 1973; *Patterns of Fashion. Englishwomen's Dresses and their construction c. 1660–1940*, (2 vols.), 1972

Boehn, M. Von, *Modes and Manners*, Vols. 1–4, Harrap, 1932–5

Boucher, F., *A History of Costume in the West*, Thames and Hudson, 1967

Brooke, I., *English Costume of the Age of Elizabeth*, Black, 1964; *English Costume of the Seventeenth Century*, Black, 1964

Bruhn, W. and Tilke, M., *A Pictorial History of Costume*, Zwemmer, 1955

Clayton, M., *Catalogue of Rubbings of Brasses and Incised Slabs;* Victoria and Albert Museum, H.M.S.O., 1968

Corson, R., *Fashions in Makeup*, Peter Owen, 1972

Courtais, C. De, *Women's Headdress and Hairstyles in England. A.D. 600 to the Present Day*, Batsford, 1973

Cunnington, C.W. and P. E., *Handbook of English Costume in the Seventeenth Century*, Faber, 1954

Cunnington, C.W., P. E. and Beard, C., *A Dictionary of English Costume*, Black, 1972

Cunnington, P. E. and Buck, A., *Children's Costume in England, 1300–1900*, Black, 1965

Davenport, M., *The Book of Costume* (2 vols.), Crown Publishers Inc., New York, 1968

Evans, M., *Costume throughout the Ages*, J. B. Lippincott Co., Philadelphia, 1950

Ewing, E., *Fashion in Underwear*, Batsford, 1971

Hill, M. H. and Bucknell, P. A., *The Evolution of Fashion,* Batsford, 1967

Hottenroth, F., *Le Costume chez les Peuples Anciens et Modernes*, 2 vols. Armand Guerinet, 1884–91. Printed E. Weyhe, New York, 1947

Kelly, F. M. and Schwabe, R., *Historic Costume, 1490–1790*, Batsford, 1929; *A Short History of Costume and Armour, 1066–1800*, Newton Abbot, 1972

Kohler, C. and Sichart, E. Von, *A History of Costume*, Harrap, 1928. Dover paperback, 1963

Kybalová, L., Hebenová, O. and Lamarová, M., *A Pictorial Encyclopaedia of Fashion*, Hamlyn, 1968

Laver, J., *Costume*, Cassell, 1963; *A Concise History of Costume*, Thames and Hudson, 1969

Waugh, N., *Corsets and Crinolines*, Batsford, 1970

Wilcox, R. T., *The Dictionary of Costume*, Batsford, 1970

Wilson, E., *History of Shoe Fashion*, Pitman, 1969

Yarwood, D., *English Costume*, Batsford, 1975; *Outline of English Costumes*, Batsford, 1967

Index

Accessories 20, 34, 51, 60
Apron 34

Baldrick 10, 11
Band 15, 25, 28, 29
   falling 15, 39; neck 15;
   standing 15; strings 15
Basque 9, 24, 25
Beard 7, 20, 50, 51
Bellypiece 9, 10
Belt 10, 11, 23, 25, 44
   shoulder 10
   sword 10
Beret 19
Bertha 25, 51
Bodice 22, 23, 24, 25, 51, 53, 54
Boots 17, 18, 26, 44, 47, 48, 54
   bucket 18
   buskins 18, 54
   jack 47, 48
   postillion 44
Bows 8, 17, 20, 32, 48, 58
Breeches 8, 11, 12, 15, 16, 17,
18, 35, 42, 44
   cloakbag 16, 17
   closed 42
   galigaskins 16
   long-legged 17
   open 16, 17, 44
   petticoat 17, 42, 44
   rhinegrave 42
   slops 16
   Spanish 16
   Venetians 16
Buckles 18, 44, 47, 48, 54
Bustle 53
   Cul de Paris 53
Buttons 10, 11, 12, 16, 17, 19,
21, 22, 23, 26, 35, 38, 47, 51
   button holes 10, 11, 38
   button and loops 10, 24

Cane 51, 60
Canions 16, 44
Cannons 44
Cap 19, 28, 32, 34, 49, 50, 54, 57
   Monmouth 20
   night 20, 49, 50
   skull 50
Cape 14, 25, 26, 28, 54
Caul 32
Chains 21
Chemise 22, 25, 26, 51, 53, 54
Chin-clout 34
Chopine 26
Cloaks 12, 14, 26, 39
   Dutch 14
   French 12
   manteau à reitre 12
   Spanish 14
Clogs 19
Coat 9, 11, 12, 26, 35, 38, 39,
44, 54
   buff 11
Cockers 19
Codpiece 16
Coif 26, 31, 57
Collar 7, 10, 11, 12, 14, 20, 22,
23, 24, 25, 35, 39, 54
   falling 11, 12
   high-standing 11, 12
   standing 22, 24
   turned-down 12, 14, 39
Comb 51
Commode 56
Corset 7, 10
Cosmetics 34
Cravat 39, 54
   Steinkirk 54
Cuff 11, 12, 15, 21, 23, 26, 35,
38, 39, 42, 44, 47, 54

Décolletage 7, 8, 22, 25, 51

Doublet 9, 10, 11, 12, 16, 23,
24, 35, 38
   peascod 9

Earrings 21, 32, 51
Echelles 51
Edging 7
Eyelets 10, 11, 16, 25

Fan 23, 24, 60
Farthingale 7, 22, 23, 24
   wheel 24
Fastening 9, 10, 11, 14, 15, 18,
24, 25, 28, 35, 39, 47, 57
Fill-in 22
Flap 16, 25
Flounces 54
Fontange 56, 57

Galoshes 19
Gamashes 19
Garters 17, 44
Girdle 25
Girdlestead 9
Gloves 18, 20, 21, 34, 51, 60
Gorget 25, 54
Gown 22, 24, 25, 35, 53

Handkerchief 21, 34, 51, 60
Hair 20, 21, 31, 32, 34, 49, 50,
56, 58
Hairstyles 8, 20, 28, 29, 31, 32,
34, 50, 58
   hurluberlu 58
   Tours 58
Hats 8, 28, 29, 31, 32, 48, 49,
50, 57
   cavalier 31
   copotain 48
   hat band 31
   Monmouth cock 49
   sugar loaf 31, 48
   tricorne 49

Headdress 50, 54
Headwear 19, 26, 48, 56
Heels 17, 18, 19, 26, 44, 45, 47, 48, 54
Hood 26, 28, 29, 32, 54, 57
  bongrace 26, 27
  chaperon 57
  French 26
  Mary Stuart 26
Hooks and Eyes 10, 23, 25
Hose 15, 17, 44
  boot 17, 44
  Spanish 17
  stirrup 17, 44
  trunk 15, 16

Jacket 8, 11, 23, 35, 39
Jerkin 11

Kirtle 22

Lace 7, 10, 12, 14, 17, 18, 21, 22, 26, 28, 32, 34, 47, 53, 54, 56, 58
Lacing 12, 18, 22, 25, 47, 51
Lapel 24
Lappets 54, 57
Leggings 19, 47
Legwear 21, 26, 42
Lockets 21

Make-up 21, 51
Mask 34
  loo mask 34
Mirror 23, 51
Mittens 21, 60
Moustache 20, 50, 51
Muckinder 21
Muff 21, 34, 51, 60
Muffler 34
Mules 19, 48

Neckband 15
Neckcloth 39
Neckerchief 25
Neckline 11, 23, 24, 25, 35
Neckwear 15, 25, 39, 54
Négligée 24
Net 32

Outer garments 22, 39

Overcoat 12, 26, 39
  brandenburg 39
  cassock 12, 39
  gaberdine 12
  jumpjacket 39
  mandilion 12
Overskirt 53

Palatine 54
Panes 10, 11, 25
Pantoffles 19, 48
Patch 21, 51
Pattens 26, 48
Perfume pads 18, 21, 34, 44, 47, 60
Petticoat 8, 22, 23, 24, 42, 54
Pinner 25
Placket holes 17
Pocket 10, 17, 18, 35, 39
Points 10, 12, 17, 18
Pomander 23
Pumps 18
Purse 21

Revers 24
Ribbon 7, 8, 10, 16, 17, 18, 19, 21, 23, 32, 35, 47, 49, 57
  bows 22, 32, 34, 39, 47, 51
  knots 18, 56, 58
  loops 18, 35, 39, 42, 44, 51, 53, 60
  ties 16, 23
Rings 21
Rosette 18, 20, 47, 48
Ruff 15, 24, 25
  falling band 15, 25
  gollila 15
  hand 15, 22, 23, 26
  standing band 15, 25
Ruffles 8, 15, 39

Sash 24
Scarf 21, 54, 60
Shawl 22
Shirt 10, 11, 12, 22, 25, 35, 39
Shoes 17, 18, 26, 44, 45, 47, 48, 54
  overshoes 19
  shoe roses 18
Shoulder knots 39
Skirt 8, 9, 10, 11, 12, 16, 22, 23, 24, 26, 35, 39, 42, 53, 54

Slashing 10, 17, 18
Sleeves 8, 10, 11, 12, 22, 23, 24, 25, 26, 35, 38, 39, 51, 53, 54
  cannon 22
  close fitting 10, 23, 39
  full 10, 25
  hanging 11, 12, 23, 24
  leg-of-mutton 23
  loose 11
  puffed out 10
Slippers 48, 54
Slits 10, 12, 23
Snuff box 51
Soles 17, 18, 19, 26, 45
Spattersashes 47
Spur leather 19, 47
Startups 18
Stirrup 19
Stockings 15, 17, 44, 47, 54
  overstockings 17
Stomacher 7, 22, 25, 54
Suit 8

Tabs 9, 10, 18, 22, 24, 25, 44, 48
Tassel 8, 21, 60
Tights 15
Tippet 26, 54
Tucker 25

Under doublet 11, 12
Underpropper 15
Under-skirt 24, 53, 54

Vamps 47
Veil 28
Vent 12, 16, 17, 35, 38, 39

Waistband 16, 42
Waistbelt 10, 51
Waistcoat 9, 11, 35
Waistline 7, 10, 11, 12, 16, 22, 25, 28, 35, 39
Welts 10, 11, 12
Whisk 54
Wigs 8, 21, 32, 49, 50
  campaign 50
  full bottomed 50
  periwigs 50
Wings 10, 11, 12, 23, 24
Wristwear 15, 25